How We Use

Plastic

Chris Oxlade

Raintree
Chicago, Illinois

© 2004 Raintree
Published by Raintree, a division of Reed Elsevier, Inc.
Chicago, IL 60602
Customer Service 888-363-4266
Visit our website at www.raintreelibrary.com

For more information address the publisher:
Raintree, 100 N. LaSalle, Suite 1200, Chicago IL 60602

Printed and bound in China by the South China
   Printing Company.

08 07 06 05
10 9 8 7 6 5 4 3 2 1

**Library of Congress Cataloging-in-Publication
Data:**
Oxlade, Chris.
  How we use plastic / Chris Oxlade.
     p. cm. -- (Using materials)
Includes bibliographical references and index.
Contents: Plastic and its properties -- Where does
plastic come from? -- Plastic parts -- Plastic containers -
- Plastics in buildings -- Plastic fibers and fabrics --
Plastics for protection -- Expanded plastics --
Plastics, heat, and electricity -- Squashy plastics --
Plastic sheets -- High-tech plastics.
  ISBN 1-4109-0596-9 (hc) 1-4109-0995-6 (pb)
  1. Plastics--Juvenile literature. [1. Plastics.] I. Title. II.
Series: Oxlade, Chris. Using materials
  TP1125.O846 2004
  668.4--dc21
                                    2003007358

Acknowledgments
The publishers would like to thank the following for
permission to reproduce photographs:
p.4 Robert Lifson/Heinemann Library; p.5 Mark S.
Skalny/Visuals Unlimited; p.6, 8 Pablo Corral/Corbis;
p.7 Stone/Getty Images; p.9 Vo Dung/SYGMA/Corbis;
pp.10, 12 Yves Tzaud; pp.11, 29 Greg
Williams/Heinemann Library; pp.13, 20 Peter Kubal;
pp.14, 27 Maximillian Stock Ltd./Science Photo
Library; p.15 Dwight Kuhn; p.16 Jonah Calinawan;
pp.17, 19 CB Productions/Corbis; pp.18, 22 Mike
French/Meonshore Studios Ltd.; pp. 21, 25, 28 J.A.
Giordano/SABA/Corbis; p.23 Tom Pantages; p.24 Jeff J.
Daly/Visuals Unlimited; p.26 The Image Bank/Getty
Images.

Cover photographs reproduced with permission of
Corbis (top) and Getty Images (Howard Kingsnorth)
(bottom).

Every effort has been made to contact copyright
holders of any material reproduced in this book.
Any omissions will be rectified in subsequent printings
if notice is given to the publishers.

Contents

Any words appearing in bold, **like this,** are explained in the Glossary.

Plastic and Its Properties

All the things we use at home, school, and work are made from materials. Plastic is a material. We use plastics for many different jobs. You can see plastics almost everywhere you look. We use them to make bags, boxes, packaging, clothes, toys, and thousands of parts for machines.

All the parts of this toy are made of plastic. Each part might be made with a different sort of plastic.

These plastic straws are made from soft, bendable plastic.

Properties tell us what a material is like. There are many different sorts of plastic. Each one has its own properties. Some plastics are very hard and strong. Others are soft and easy to bend. Some plastics get soft when they are heated up. Other plastics stay hard. Almost all plastics are light and last a long time.

Don't use it!

*The different properties of materials make them useful for different jobs. These properties can also make them unsuitable for some jobs. For example, most plastics **melt** when they get very hot. So we cannot use plastic to make ovens.*

Where Does Plastic Come From?

Plastics are not **natural** materials. They are **artificial** materials made in factories. Plastics are made from **chemicals.** We get the chemicals from natural materials such as crude oil, gas, and coal. These are called fossil fuels. These are fuels that have formed over millions of years from the remains of dead plants and animals. Sometimes we get chemicals for plastics from rocks or plants, such as cotton.

The **raw materials** needed for making plastics can come from deep under the ground. This rig is drilling for oil under the ocean floor.

This is what a strip of film looks like under a **microscope**. This film is made from plastic.

Crude oil, gas, and coal are split up into many chemicals. Then the chemicals can be used to make different kinds of plastics. Most plastics come out of the factory in chips and **granules,** ready to be made into things.

The first plastic

*The first plastic was made more than 100 years ago. It was called celluloid because it was made from a chemical called cellulose. It was used to make film for cameras. We get cellulose from wood. Celluloid has been replaced by modern plastics with more useful **properties.***

Plastic Parts

Plastic is easy to make into objects of many different sizes and shapes. We use it to make things from tiny parts of machines to whole tables and chairs. Plastic parts are tough and long-lasting. They are also cheap to make. Small things, such as plastic cups and spoons, are so cheap that we often use them once and throw them away. We say that they are **disposable.**

Plastic is a good material for things we use outdoors. Plastic does not **rot** like wood, or **rust** like metal.

Molding parts

By using molds, we can make lots of plastic objects that are exactly the same.

Plastic parts are made in **molds.** A mold is a block of metal with a space inside. The space is the shape of the object that is going to be made. Plastic is heated until it **melts** and then poured into the mold. When the plastic has cooled down and hardened, the mold is opened and the part is taken out. Every plastic part made in a mold is exactly the same shape.

9

Plastic Containers

Many plastics do not let water or air flow through them. They are **waterproof** and **airtight.** These **properties** make plastics good materials for containers. We make soda bottles, storage boxes, trash cans, bowls, and buckets from plastic. Some special plastic food containers can be put in an oven without **melting.**

Soda bottles are made from a strong plastic called polyethylene terephthalate (PET for short).

These plastic containers are used with takeout meals to keep sauces warm.

Plastic instead of glass

Many containers, such as bottles and drinking glasses, are made from glass. Glass is a **brittle** material. Glass containers break easily if they are dropped. Plastic can bend without snapping, so plastic containers do not usually break if they are dropped. We use plastic for containers that need to be strong, such as baby bottles.

Don't use it!
*Most plastics are affected by **chemicals**. For example, some **acids** can eat away plastic. When we cannot store chemicals such as acid in plastic containers, we have to use glass containers instead.*

Plastics in Buildings

Builders use plastics when they build houses and other buildings. Window frames, door frames, and gutters are often made of plastic. So are pipes that carry away rainwater, and pipes that carry away waste water from baths, showers, and toilets. All these things are made from a plastic called polyvinyl chloride (PVC for short).

The plastic parts of this window frame were joined by heating their ends to make them stick together.

Plastic pipes can last hundreds of years.

We sometimes use plastic instead of wood for window frames because plastic does not **rot** like wood. Some people prefer wood, though, because it looks more **natural** than plastic. We do not need to put **preservatives** or paint on plastic. We use plastic instead of metal for pipes because plastic does not **rust** like metal.

Don't use it!

Some plastics are strong, but they are not strong enough to hold up a building. So we cannot use plastics for the main parts of a house, such as the walls and the roof. We need to use very strong materials for buildings, such as brick, steel, and concrete instead.

Plastic Fibers and Fabrics

A **fiber** is a thin strand of material. The hairs on your head are fibers. Plastic fibers are stronger than **natural** fibers, such as cotton and wool. Plastic fibers are made by pushing hot, soft plastic through tiny holes. The most common plastic fibers are called polyester, acrylic, and polypropylene.

This is what plastic netting looks like through a **microscope**. You can see the fibers twisted together.

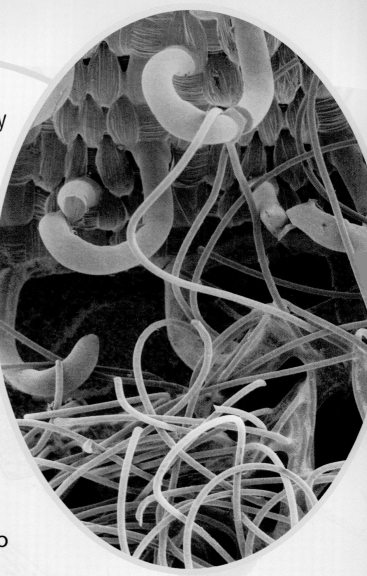

Velcro is made from tiny plastic loops and hooks.

Polyester fibers and acrylic fibers are woven together to make **fabrics.** Polyester fabrics are made into clothes, such as shirts and waterproof jackets. Clothes made from acrylic fabrics do not get creases in them.

Waterproof fabrics

Some fabrics are made from sheets of plastic. For example, chairs are sometimes covered with sheets of PVC fabric. The fabric often has a pattern on it to make it look like leather. We also put PVC on woven fabrics to make them **waterproof.**

Plastics for Protection

Some sorts of plastic are extremely tough. They bend a little bit, but they are very hard to break. We use tough plastics to make containers for delicate equipment. For example, computers, cell phones, and radios have hard cases made from a tough plastic called ABS. If you drop them accidentally the plastic doesn't usually break.

The lenses in these sunglasses are made from tough polycarbonate. They should not break or scratch.

The plastic used to make this safety helmet is very tough.

We make safety equipment from tough plastics, too. For example, safety goggles are made of acrylic. They do not shatter into pieces if something hits them or they are dropped. Safety helmets for people on building sites or motorcycle drivers are usually made from ABS plastic. They protect people's heads from falling objects.

Plastics, Heat, and Electricity

Heat cannot flow through plastics very well. If you put a plastic spoon in a hot drink the spoon's handle stays cool. Only the part of the spoon that touches the hot drink will heat up. We often use plastic for pan handles because the plastic stays cool when the pan is hot. Plastic does not **conduct** heat well.

Plastic spoons can get soft if they are put in boiling water.

The electronic parts inside machines are joined to a kind of plastic that does not melt if it gets hot.

Most plastics get soft when they get hot. Scientists call these plastics thermoplastics. When thermoplastics cool down they get hard again. Some plastics do not get soft when they get hot. Scientists call these plastics thermosetting plastics. We use thermosetting plastics to make things that might get hot. For example, electric plugs and sockets are made of thermosetting plastics.

Electricity cannot flow through plastics, either. We cover metal wires that carry electricity with plastic called PVC. The plastic stops electricity from jumping from one wire to another by accident.

Plastics for Packaging

Some plastics are very light. This is because they are full of millions of tiny air bubbles. Filling a piece of plastic with bubbles makes it expand so it is bigger. We call these kinds of plastic expanded plastic or foamed plastic.

The most common expanded plastic is called expanded polystyrene. It is the white plastic that is used to protect things, such as televisions, inside their packing boxes.

This is what expanded polystyrene looks like under a microscope. You can see the tiny bubbles inside.

Takeout food boxes are good because they are light to carry.

Insulating

We also use expanded plastic for food containers. Hot drinks, sandwiches, and burgers often come in boxes made from expanded plastic. The tiny bubbles inside the plastic **insulate** the food. This keeps the food warm and keeps your fingers from getting hot!

Don't use it!

Many cushions and mattresses are made from expanded plastic called polyurethane foam. It is soft, bendable, and light. This plastic burns very easily, so we cannot use this sort of plastic where it might catch fire.

Rubbery Plastics

Some types of plastic are rubbery. You can squash or stretch things made from rubbery plastics. They always go back into their original shape afterward. Rubber was once made only from **natural** rubber, which comes from trees. Today it is usually made from rubbery plastic or a mixture of natural rubber and plastic. There is not enough natural rubber for all the rubber the world uses.

Some toys are made specially to be squeezed.

Wetsuits used by divers are made from neoprene. This close-up photograph shows the bubbles in neoprene. They help to stop heat from moving through the material.

Don't use it!

We cannot use squashy, rubbery plastics in places where we do not want them to stretch. For example, we would not use a rubbery plastic to make a soda bottle. The sides would stretch and the bottle would fall over.

The main use of rubbery plastics is for making tires for cars, trucks, bikes, and buses. The rubber tires give passengers a smooth ride over bumps in the road. Tires also grip the road to stop wheels from sliding. We also use rubbery plastics to make soft soles for shoes and boots.

Plastic Sheets

Plastic sheets are light, bendable, **waterproof,** and **airtight.** We make plastic sheets into many different products. Millions of plastic bags are made from sheets of a plastic called polyethylene. They are light, strong, waterproof, and cheap. We use plastic bags for hundreds of jobs such as carrying groceries, storing food, and collecting trash.

Bubble wrap is made from two sheets of plastic glued together with air bubbles trapped between them.

Candy wrappers are made from small pieces of plastic sheet.

We make plastic bags by blowing air into hot, liquid plastic. This blows the plastic up into a huge, long tube. When the plastic cools down it is cut into short tubes. One end of a short tube is heated up to join the sides together and make a bag.

We also make plastic sheets to wrap food and candy, for shower curtains, for drink containers, and to cover things to protect them from water and dirt.

High-Tech Plastics

Scientists are **inventing** new plastics with special **properties** all the time. They might be very hard, very strong, very light, or stay hard when they get very hot. For example, a plastic called PTFE has a very slippery surface. It is also tough and does not **melt** even when it gets very hot. These properties make it good for non-stick pans.

This pan has a non-stick coating of PTFE plastic. PTFE is short for polytetrafluoroethylene.

This special
liquid is used to
hold the different materials
in a composite material together.

Plastics and other materials

Some materials are made from plastic mixed with other substances. These materials are called **composites.** A composite material has the properties of both materials. For example, a material called glass-reinforced plastic (GRP for short) is made up of plastic mixed with thin glass **fibers.** The glass fibers make the GRP very strong.

Plastic and the Environment

Plastics do not **rot** or **rust.** This means that plastic objects such as rain gutters last a long time. It also means that plastic trash will not **rot** away, either. When we throw plastics away we also waste the **chemicals** that the plastics were made from. Most of the chemicals come from oil. If we do not reuse oil it will eventually run out because it cannot be replaced.

When we throw away plastic things, they sit for hundreds of years in the environment.

Recycling bins are provided in most areas, making recycling very easy.

Recycling plastics

We can help the environment by using plastics again instead of throwing them away. This is called recycling. Recycling helps to keep us from using up all of the world's precious oil. Some sorts of plastic can be **melted** to make new plastic.

29

Find Out for Yourself

The best way to find out more about plastics is to investigate plastics for yourself. Look around your home and school for plastics. Think about why plastic was used for each job. What **properties** make it the right material for the job? You will find the answers to many of your questions in this book. You can also look in other books and on the Internet.

Books to read

Ballard, Carol. *Science Answers: Grouping Materials: From Gold to Wool*. Chicago: Heinemann Library, 2003.

Hunter, Rebecca. *Discovering Science: Matter*. Chicago: Raintree, 2001.

Using the Internet

Try searching the Internet to find out about things having to do with plastics. Websites can change, so if one of the links below no longer works, don't worry. Use a search engine, such as www.yahooligans.com or www.internet4kids.com. For example, you could try searching using the keywords "thermoplastic," "polycarbonate," and "plastic bottles."

Websites

http://www.bbc.co.uk/schools/revisewise/science/materials/
A great site that explains all about different materials.

www.epa.gov/recyclecity
Learn more about recycling. Includes games, activities, facts, and graphics.

Glossary

acid liquid that can eat away at materials

airtight describes a material that does not let air pass through it

artificial describes a material that is not found naturally. It is made by people.

brittle describes a material that snaps or breaks apart easily

chemical substance that we use to make other substances, or for jobs such as cleaning

composite material made from two other materials used together. For example, glass-reinforced plastic is made from glass and plastic.

conduct to let heat or electricity pass through

disposable describes an object that is made to be thrown away after it is used

electricity form of energy that flows along wires

fabric cloth or other material

fiber long, thin, bendable piece of material

granule small lump of a material

insulate stop heat from escaping

invent make something for the first time

melt turn from a solid into a liquid by heating

microscope instrument used for looking at things in tiny detail. Microscopes make things look much larger.

mold block of metal with a space in the center. When melted plastic is poured into the mold, it sets, making an object the same shape as the inside of the mold.

natural describes anything that is not made by people

preservative chemical that helps to stop a material from rotting

property quality of a material that tell us what it is like. Hard, soft, bendable, and strong are all properties.

raw material natural material that is used to make other materials

rot to break down into a simpler material

rust process that makes iron and steel weak and crumbly. It happens when iron or steel is left in damp air or water.

waterproof describes a material that does not let water pass through it

Index